50 Delicious Noodle Recipes for Home

By: Kelly Johnson

Table of Contents

- Classic Ramen
- Pad Thai
- Lo Mein
- Pho (Vietnamese Noodle Soup)
- Dan Dan Noodles
- Chow Mein
- Japchae (Korean Glass Noodles)
- Laksa (Spicy Coconut Noodle Soup)
- Singapore Noodles
- Yaki Udon
- Drunken Noodles (Pad Kee Mao)
- Soba Noodle Salad
- Cold Sesame Noodles
- Miso Udon Soup
- Chicken Yakisoba
- Spicy Sichuan Noodles
- Peanut Noodles
- Korean Jajangmyeon (Black Bean Noodles)
- Thai Green Curry Noodles
- Char Kway Teow
- Classic Spaghetti Bolognese
- Fettuccine Alfredo
- Carbonara
- Lasagna
- Pesto Pasta
- Cacio e Pepe
- Seafood Linguine
- Pasta Primavera
- Baked Ziti
- Gnocchi with Brown Butter Sauce
- Tagliatelle with Truffle Cream
- Tortellini Soup
- Pappardelle with Short Rib Ragu
- Penne Arrabbiata
- Mac and Cheese

- Spaghetti Aglio e Olio
- Vodka Pasta
- Mushroom Stroganoff
- Hungarian Nokedli (Dumpling Noodles)
- Greek Orzo Salad
- Chicken Noodle Soup
- Beef Stroganoff
- Filipino Pancit Canton
- Burmese Coconut Noodles
- Moroccan Harira Soup with Vermicelli
- Egyptian Kushari
- Spätzle (German Egg Noodles)
- Venezuelan Tallarines with Meat Sauce
- Peruvian Tallarines Verdes
- Tunisian Lablabi with Noodles

Classic Ramen (Japanese Noodle Soup)

Ingredients:

- 4 cups chicken or pork broth
- 2 tbsp soy sauce
- 1 tbsp miso paste
- 1 tsp sesame oil
- 2 packs fresh or dried ramen noodles
- 1 soft-boiled egg, halved
- ½ cup sliced green onions
- ½ cup bamboo shoots (optional)
- 4 slices chashu pork (or cooked chicken)
- ½ sheet nori (seaweed)

Instructions:

1. Heat broth, soy sauce, miso, and sesame oil in a pot.
2. Cook noodles separately, then drain.
3. Pour broth over noodles in a bowl.
4. Top with egg, pork, green onions, bamboo shoots, and nori.

Pad Thai (Thai Stir-Fried Noodles)

Ingredients:

- 8 oz rice noodles
- 2 tbsp oil
- 1 cup shrimp or chicken (optional)
- 2 eggs, beaten
- ½ cup bean sprouts
- ¼ cup crushed peanuts
- 2 green onions, sliced
- 1 lime, cut into wedges

Sauce:

- 3 tbsp fish sauce
- 1 tbsp tamarind paste
- 1 tbsp sugar
- ½ tsp chili flakes

Instructions:

1. Soak noodles in warm water until soft, then drain.
2. Stir-fry protein in oil, then add eggs and scramble.
3. Add noodles, sauce, and bean sprouts. Stir-fry for 2 minutes.
4. Garnish with peanuts, green onions, and lime.

Lo Mein (Chinese Stir-Fried Noodles)

Ingredients:

- 8 oz egg noodles
- 2 tbsp oil
- 1 cup mixed vegetables (carrots, bell peppers, snow peas)
- 1 cup chicken, beef, or tofu (optional)
- 2 garlic cloves, minced

Sauce:

- 2 tbsp soy sauce
- 1 tbsp oyster sauce
- 1 tsp sesame oil
- 1 tsp sugar

Instructions:

1. Cook noodles and set aside.
2. Stir-fry protein and vegetables in oil.
3. Add noodles and sauce, tossing to coat.

Pho (Vietnamese Noodle Soup)

Ingredients:

- 4 cups beef broth
- 1 cinnamon stick
- 3 star anise
- 1 tbsp fish sauce
- 1 tbsp sugar
- 8 oz rice noodles
- ½ lb thinly sliced beef
- ½ cup bean sprouts
- ½ cup fresh basil
- ½ lime, cut into wedges

Instructions:

1. Simmer broth with cinnamon, star anise, fish sauce, and sugar for 30 minutes.
2. Cook noodles and place in a bowl.
3. Pour hot broth over raw beef slices and noodles.
4. Serve with bean sprouts, basil, and lime.

Dan Dan Noodles (Spicy Sichuan Noodles)

Ingredients:

- 8 oz wheat noodles
- ½ lb ground pork
- 1 tbsp chili oil
- 1 tbsp Sichuan peppercorns
- 1 tbsp soy sauce
- 1 tbsp black vinegar
- 2 tbsp peanut butter or tahini
- 1 tbsp garlic, minced
- 1 green onion, chopped

Instructions:

1. Cook noodles and set aside.
2. Sauté pork with chili oil and garlic.
3. Mix soy sauce, vinegar, peanut butter, and Sichuan peppercorns into a sauce.
4. Toss noodles with sauce and top with pork and green onions.

Chow Mein (Crispy Stir-Fried Noodles)

Ingredients:

- 8 oz egg noodles
- 2 tbsp oil
- 1 cup cabbage, shredded
- ½ cup carrots, julienned
- ½ cup bean sprouts
- 1 tbsp soy sauce
- 1 tsp sesame oil

Instructions:

1. Boil noodles, then pan-fry until crispy.
2. Stir-fry veggies, then toss with noodles and sauce.

Japchae (Korean Glass Noodles)

Ingredients:

- 8 oz sweet potato glass noodles
- 1 cup beef or mushrooms, sliced
- 1 carrot, julienned
- ½ onion, sliced
- 1 cup spinach
- 2 tbsp soy sauce
- 1 tbsp sesame oil
- 1 tsp sugar

Instructions:

1. Cook noodles and set aside.
2. Stir-fry beef, onion, and carrot.
3. Toss everything together with soy sauce, sesame oil, and sugar.

Laksa (Spicy Coconut Noodle Soup)

Ingredients:

- 4 cups chicken or shrimp broth
- 1 can coconut milk
- 2 tbsp red curry paste
- 8 oz rice noodles
- 1 cup shrimp or chicken
- ½ cup bean sprouts
- 1 lime, cut into wedges
- Fresh cilantro for garnish

Instructions:

1. Simmer broth, coconut milk, and curry paste.
2. Cook noodles separately, then add to the soup.
3. Add shrimp and simmer for 3 minutes.
4. Serve with bean sprouts, lime, and cilantro.

Singapore Noodles (Curry Stir-Fried Noodles)

Ingredients:

- 8 oz rice vermicelli noodles
- 1 tbsp curry powder
- 1 tbsp soy sauce
- 1 cup shrimp or chicken
- 1 cup mixed veggies (bell peppers, carrots, onions)
- 1 tbsp oil

Instructions:

1. Soak noodles in warm water, then drain.
2. Stir-fry protein and vegetables in oil.
3. Add noodles, curry powder, and soy sauce. Toss to combine.

Yaki Udon (Japanese Stir-Fried Udon)

Ingredients:

- 8 oz udon noodles
- 2 tbsp oil
- 1 cup mushrooms, sliced
- ½ cup cabbage, shredded
- 1 tbsp soy sauce
- 1 tbsp oyster sauce
- 1 tsp sesame oil

Instructions:

1. Cook udon noodles and drain.
2. Stir-fry mushrooms and cabbage, then add noodles and sauce.

Drunken Noodles (Pad Kee Mao)

Ingredients:

- 8 oz wide rice noodles
- 2 tbsp oil
- 1 cup chicken or tofu
- 2 garlic cloves, minced
- ½ cup bell peppers, sliced
- ½ cup Thai basil
- 1 tbsp soy sauce
- 1 tbsp oyster sauce
- 1 tsp chili flakes

Instructions:

1. Cook noodles and set aside.
2. Stir-fry garlic, chicken, and peppers.
3. Toss in noodles, sauces, and basil.

Soba Noodle Salad

Ingredients:

- 8 oz soba noodles
- 1 cup shredded carrots
- ½ cup sliced cucumbers
- ¼ cup green onions
- 2 tbsp sesame oil
- 1 tbsp soy sauce
- 1 tbsp rice vinegar
- 1 tsp sesame seeds

Instructions:

1. Cook soba noodles, rinse in cold water.
2. Toss with vegetables and dressing.

Cold Sesame Noodles (Chinese Chilled Noodles)

Ingredients:

- 8 oz wheat or egg noodles
- 2 tbsp sesame paste or peanut butter
- 1 tbsp soy sauce
- 1 tbsp rice vinegar
- 1 tbsp sesame oil
- 1 tsp chili oil (optional)
- 1 garlic clove, minced
- 1 tsp sugar
- 1 green onion, sliced
- 1 tbsp sesame seeds

Instructions:

1. Cook noodles, rinse under cold water, and drain.
2. Mix sesame paste, soy sauce, vinegar, sesame oil, chili oil, garlic, and sugar.
3. Toss noodles with sauce and garnish with green onions and sesame seeds.

Miso Udon Soup (Japanese Comfort Noodle Soup)

Ingredients:

- 4 cups dashi (or vegetable broth)
- 2 tbsp miso paste
- 8 oz udon noodles
- 1 cup mushrooms, sliced
- ½ cup tofu, cubed
- 1 green onion, chopped
- 1 tbsp soy sauce
- ½ sheet nori (optional)

Instructions:

1. Heat dashi broth, then dissolve miso paste in a small amount of warm broth before adding it back.
2. Add mushrooms, tofu, and soy sauce, simmer for 5 minutes.
3. Cook udon separately, then add to the soup.
4. Garnish with green onions and nori.

Chicken Yakisoba (Japanese Stir-Fried Noodles)

Ingredients:

- 8 oz yakisoba noodles
- 1 chicken breast, sliced
- 1 cup cabbage, shredded
- ½ cup carrots, julienned
- 2 tbsp soy sauce
- 1 tbsp oyster sauce
- 1 tbsp Worcestershire sauce
- 1 tbsp oil
- 1 green onion, sliced

Instructions:

1. Cook noodles and set aside.
2. Stir-fry chicken in oil, then add cabbage and carrots.
3. Add noodles and sauce, tossing to combine.

Spicy Sichuan Noodles

Ingredients:

- 8 oz wheat noodles
- 2 tbsp chili oil
- 1 tbsp soy sauce
- 1 tbsp black vinegar
- 1 tsp Sichuan peppercorns, ground
- 1 garlic clove, minced
- 1 tbsp green onions, sliced

Instructions:

1. Cook noodles and drain.
2. Toss with chili oil, soy sauce, vinegar, peppercorns, and garlic.
3. Garnish with green onions.

Peanut Noodles

Ingredients:

- 8 oz rice noodles
- 2 tbsp peanut butter
- 1 tbsp soy sauce
- 1 tbsp rice vinegar
- 1 tsp sesame oil
- 1 tsp honey
- 1 garlic clove, minced
- 1 tbsp chopped peanuts

Instructions:

1. Cook noodles and drain.
2. Mix peanut butter, soy sauce, vinegar, sesame oil, honey, and garlic into a sauce.
3. Toss noodles with sauce and garnish with peanuts.

Korean Jajangmyeon (Black Bean Noodles)

Ingredients:

- 8 oz thick wheat noodles
- ½ lb pork belly or ground pork
- 1 cup zucchini, diced
- ½ cup potato, diced
- ½ cup onion, chopped
- 3 tbsp chunjang (Korean black bean paste)
- 1 tbsp sugar
- 1 tbsp oil

Instructions:

1. Stir-fry pork, onion, zucchini, and potato in oil.
2. Add black bean paste and sugar, stir-fry for 2 minutes.
3. Cook noodles, drain, and toss with sauce.

Thai Green Curry Noodles

Ingredients:

- 8 oz rice noodles
- 2 tbsp green curry paste
- 1 cup coconut milk
- 1 cup chicken or tofu
- ½ cup bell peppers, sliced
- 1 tbsp fish sauce
- 1 lime, cut into wedges
- Fresh cilantro for garnish

Instructions:

1. Cook noodles and drain.
2. Simmer green curry paste, coconut milk, and fish sauce.
3. Add chicken and peppers, cook for 5 minutes.
4. Toss with noodles and garnish with lime and cilantro.

Char Kway Teow (Malaysian Stir-Fried Flat Noodles)

Ingredients:

- 8 oz flat rice noodles
- ½ cup shrimp
- ½ cup Chinese sausage, sliced
- 1 egg, beaten
- ½ cup bean sprouts
- 2 tbsp dark soy sauce
- 1 tbsp oyster sauce
- 1 tbsp chili paste
- 1 tbsp oil

Instructions:

1. Stir-fry shrimp and sausage in oil.
2. Add noodles, sauces, and chili paste.
3. Push everything aside, scramble the egg, then mix.
4. Toss with bean sprouts.

Classic Spaghetti Bolognese

Ingredients:

- 8 oz spaghetti
- ½ lb ground beef
- 1 small onion, chopped
- 2 garlic cloves, minced
- 1 can (14 oz) crushed tomatoes
- 1 tbsp tomato paste
- 1 tsp oregano
- 1 tsp basil
- ½ cup Parmesan cheese

Instructions:

1. Cook spaghetti and set aside.
2. Brown beef with onion and garlic.
3. Add tomatoes, tomato paste, and herbs, simmer for 15 minutes.
4. Toss with pasta and top with Parmesan.

Fettuccine Alfredo

Ingredients:

- 8 oz fettuccine
- 1 cup heavy cream
- ½ cup Parmesan cheese
- 2 tbsp butter
- 1 garlic clove, minced

Instructions:

1. Cook fettuccine and drain.
2. Melt butter, sauté garlic, then add cream and cheese.
3. Toss with pasta and serve.

Carbonara (Italian Egg and Bacon Pasta)

Ingredients:

- 8 oz spaghetti
- 2 eggs
- ½ cup Parmesan cheese
- 4 oz pancetta or bacon, diced
- 1 garlic clove, minced
- Black pepper

Instructions:

1. Cook spaghetti, reserving ½ cup pasta water.
2. Sauté pancetta and garlic.
3. Whisk eggs and cheese together.
4. Toss pasta with egg mixture, adding reserved pasta water to create a creamy sauce.
5. Top with black pepper.

Lasagna

Ingredients:

- 12 lasagna noodles
- 1 lb ground beef or Italian sausage
- 1 small onion, chopped
- 2 garlic cloves, minced
- 1 can (28 oz) crushed tomatoes
- 1 cup ricotta cheese
- 2 cups shredded mozzarella
- ½ cup Parmesan cheese
- 1 egg
- 1 tsp oregano
- 1 tsp basil

Instructions:

1. Cook lasagna noodles and set aside.
2. Brown beef with onion and garlic, then add tomatoes, oregano, and basil. Simmer for 15 minutes.
3. Mix ricotta, egg, and Parmesan in a bowl.
4. Layer sauce, noodles, ricotta mixture, and mozzarella in a baking dish.
5. Bake at 375°F (190°C) for 30-40 minutes.

Pesto Pasta

Ingredients:

- 8 oz pasta (penne, spaghetti, or fusilli)
- 2 cups fresh basil leaves
- ¼ cup pine nuts
- 2 garlic cloves
- ½ cup grated Parmesan
- ⅓ cup olive oil

Instructions:

1. Cook pasta and drain.
2. Blend basil, pine nuts, garlic, Parmesan, and olive oil into a pesto.
3. Toss pasta with pesto and serve.

Cacio e Pepe

Ingredients:

- 8 oz spaghetti
- 1 cup Pecorino Romano cheese, grated
- 1 tsp black pepper, freshly ground

Instructions:

1. Cook spaghetti, reserving ½ cup pasta water.
2. Toast black pepper in a dry pan.
3. Toss pasta with cheese, black pepper, and reserved water until creamy.

Seafood Linguine

Ingredients:

- 8 oz linguine
- ½ lb shrimp, scallops, or mussels
- 2 tbsp butter
- 2 garlic cloves, minced
- ½ cup white wine
- 1 cup cherry tomatoes, halved
- ½ tsp red pepper flakes
- 2 tbsp parsley, chopped

Instructions:

1. Cook linguine and drain.
2. Sauté garlic in butter, add seafood, and cook until opaque.
3. Add wine, tomatoes, and red pepper flakes, simmer for 5 minutes.
4. Toss with pasta and parsley.

Pasta Primavera

Ingredients:

- 8 oz pasta (penne or spaghetti)
- 1 zucchini, sliced
- 1 bell pepper, sliced
- 1 cup cherry tomatoes, halved
- 2 garlic cloves, minced
- ¼ cup olive oil
- ½ cup Parmesan

Instructions:

1. Cook pasta and drain.
2. Sauté vegetables in olive oil.
3. Toss with pasta and Parmesan.

Baked Ziti

Ingredients:

- 12 oz ziti pasta
- 2 cups marinara sauce
- 1 cup ricotta cheese
- 1 cup shredded mozzarella
- ½ cup Parmesan

Instructions:

1. Cook ziti and drain.
2. Mix pasta with marinara and ricotta.
3. Transfer to a baking dish, top with mozzarella and Parmesan.
4. Bake at 375°F (190°C) for 25 minutes.

Gnocchi with Brown Butter Sauce

Ingredients:

- 1 lb potato gnocchi
- 4 tbsp butter
- 5 fresh sage leaves
- ½ cup grated Parmesan

Instructions:

1. Cook gnocchi and drain.
2. Melt butter in a pan, add sage leaves, and cook until fragrant.
3. Toss gnocchi with butter sauce and Parmesan.

Tagliatelle with Truffle Cream

Ingredients:

- 8 oz tagliatelle
- ½ cup heavy cream
- 2 tbsp truffle oil
- ½ cup grated Parmesan

Instructions:

1. Cook tagliatelle and drain.
2. Heat cream and truffle oil, then toss with pasta and Parmesan.

Tortellini Soup

Ingredients:

- 1 package (9 oz) cheese tortellini
- 4 cups chicken broth
- 1 can (14 oz) diced tomatoes
- 1 cup spinach
- 2 garlic cloves, minced
- ½ cup Parmesan

Instructions:

1. Bring broth and tomatoes to a boil.
2. Add tortellini and cook for 5 minutes.
3. Stir in spinach and garlic, then serve with Parmesan.

Pappardelle with Short Rib Ragu

Ingredients:

- 8 oz pappardelle
- 1 lb short ribs
- 1 small onion, chopped
- 2 garlic cloves, minced
- 1 can (14 oz) crushed tomatoes
- ½ cup red wine
- 1 tsp rosemary

Instructions:

1. Brown short ribs, then remove.
2. Sauté onion and garlic, then deglaze with wine.
3. Add tomatoes, rosemary, and ribs. Simmer for 2 hours.
4. Shred meat and toss with cooked pappardelle.

Penne Arrabbiata

Ingredients:

- 8 oz penne
- 2 tbsp olive oil
- 2 garlic cloves, minced
- 1 tsp red pepper flakes
- 1 can (14 oz) crushed tomatoes
- ½ cup Parmesan

Instructions:

1. Cook penne and drain.
2. Sauté garlic and red pepper flakes in oil.
3. Add tomatoes, simmer for 10 minutes.
4. Toss with pasta and Parmesan.

Mac and Cheese

Ingredients:

- 8 oz elbow macaroni
- 2 tbsp butter
- 2 tbsp flour
- 2 cups milk
- 2 cups shredded cheddar

Instructions:

1. Cook macaroni and drain.
2. Melt butter, whisk in flour, then slowly add milk.
3. Stir in cheese and toss with pasta.

Spaghetti Aglio e Olio

Ingredients:

- 8 oz spaghetti
- 3 tbsp olive oil
- 4 garlic cloves, sliced
- ½ tsp red pepper flakes
- ½ cup parsley, chopped

Instructions:

1. Cook spaghetti and drain.
2. Sauté garlic and red pepper flakes in olive oil.
3. Toss with pasta and parsley.

Vodka Pasta

Ingredients:

- 12 oz penne
- 2 tbsp olive oil
- 1 small onion, finely chopped
- 2 garlic cloves, minced
- ½ tsp red pepper flakes
- ½ cup vodka
- 1 can (14 oz) crushed tomatoes
- ½ cup heavy cream
- ½ cup Parmesan, grated

Instructions:

1. Cook penne and drain.
2. Sauté onion, garlic, and red pepper flakes in olive oil.
3. Add vodka and cook until reduced. Stir in tomatoes and simmer.
4. Add heavy cream and Parmesan, then toss with pasta.

Mushroom Stroganoff

Ingredients:

- 8 oz egg noodles
- 2 tbsp butter
- 1 lb mushrooms, sliced
- 1 small onion, chopped
- 2 garlic cloves, minced
- 1 cup vegetable broth
- 1 tbsp flour
- ½ cup sour cream
- 1 tsp Dijon mustard
- ½ tsp paprika

Instructions:

1. Cook egg noodles and drain.
2. Sauté mushrooms, onion, and garlic in butter.
3. Stir in flour, then add broth and simmer.
4. Mix in sour cream, mustard, and paprika. Toss with noodles.

Hungarian Nokedli (Dumpling Noodles)

Ingredients:

- 2 cups flour
- 2 eggs
- ½ cup water
- ½ tsp salt

Instructions:

1. Mix flour, eggs, water, and salt to form a sticky dough.
2. Drop small spoonfuls into boiling water.
3. Cook until dumplings float, then drain.

Greek Orzo Salad

Ingredients:

- 1 cup orzo
- ½ cup cherry tomatoes, halved
- ½ cup cucumber, diced
- ¼ cup red onion, chopped
- ¼ cup Kalamata olives, sliced
- ¼ cup feta cheese
- 2 tbsp olive oil
- 1 tbsp lemon juice
- ½ tsp oregano

Instructions:

1. Cook orzo and cool.
2. Toss with vegetables, olives, and feta.
3. Drizzle with olive oil, lemon juice, and oregano.

Chicken Noodle Soup

Ingredients:

- 1 lb chicken breast
- 6 cups chicken broth
- 1 small onion, chopped
- 2 carrots, sliced
- 2 celery stalks, sliced
- 2 garlic cloves, minced
- 6 oz egg noodles
- 1 tsp thyme

Instructions:

1. Sauté onion, carrots, celery, and garlic in a pot.
2. Add broth and chicken, simmer until chicken is cooked.
3. Shred chicken, return to pot, add noodles, and cook until tender.

Beef Stroganoff

Ingredients:

- 8 oz egg noodles
- 1 lb beef sirloin, sliced
- 2 tbsp butter
- 1 small onion, chopped
- 2 garlic cloves, minced
- 1 cup mushrooms, sliced
- ½ cup beef broth
- ½ cup sour cream
- 1 tbsp Dijon mustard

Instructions:

1. Cook noodles and drain.
2. Sauté beef in butter until browned. Remove and set aside.
3. Cook onion, garlic, and mushrooms. Add broth and simmer.
4. Stir in sour cream and mustard, then return beef and toss with noodles.

Filipino Pancit Canton

Ingredients:

- 8 oz pancit canton noodles
- 2 tbsp oil
- 1 small onion, chopped
- 2 garlic cloves, minced
- ½ cup chicken, sliced
- ½ cup shrimp
- 1 carrot, julienned
- 1 cup cabbage, shredded
- 2 tbsp soy sauce
- 1 tbsp oyster sauce
- ½ tsp black pepper

Instructions:

1. Sauté onion and garlic in oil. Add chicken and shrimp.
2. Stir in vegetables, soy sauce, and oyster sauce.
3. Add noodles and cook until combined.

Burmese Coconut Noodles (Ohn No Khao Swe)

Ingredients:

- 8 oz egg noodles
- 2 tbsp vegetable oil
- 1 small onion, chopped
- 2 garlic cloves, minced
- 1 tsp turmeric
- 1 tsp paprika
- 1 tbsp fish sauce
- 2 cups chicken broth
- 1 can (14 oz) coconut milk
- 1 lb chicken breast, sliced
- 1 tbsp chickpea flour (or regular flour)
- 1 boiled egg, sliced (for garnish)
- Fresh cilantro and lime wedges (for garnish)

Instructions:

1. Cook the noodles and set aside.
2. In a pot, sauté onions, garlic, turmeric, and paprika in oil.
3. Add chicken and cook until lightly browned.
4. Stir in fish sauce, broth, and coconut milk. Simmer for 10 minutes.
5. Mix chickpea flour with a little water, then add to the soup to thicken.
6. Serve over noodles and garnish with boiled egg, cilantro, and lime.

Moroccan Harira Soup with Vermicelli

Ingredients:

- 1 tbsp olive oil
- 1 small onion, chopped
- 2 garlic cloves, minced
- 1 tsp ground cumin
- ½ tsp ground cinnamon
- ½ tsp ground turmeric
- ½ tsp paprika
- 1 can (14 oz) diced tomatoes
- 4 cups vegetable broth
- ½ cup cooked chickpeas
- ½ cup cooked lentils
- 2 oz vermicelli noodles, broken into small pieces
- 1 tbsp fresh parsley, chopped
- 1 tbsp lemon juice

Instructions:

1. Heat oil in a pot and sauté onions and garlic.
2. Stir in spices and cook for 1 minute.
3. Add tomatoes, broth, chickpeas, and lentils. Simmer for 20 minutes.
4. Add vermicelli and cook until soft.
5. Stir in parsley and lemon juice before serving.

Egyptian Kushari

Ingredients:

- ½ cup lentils
- ½ cup rice
- ½ cup elbow macaroni
- 1 tbsp olive oil
- 1 onion, thinly sliced
- 1 can (14 oz) tomato sauce
- 2 garlic cloves, minced
- 1 tsp cumin
- ½ tsp red pepper flakes
- 1 tbsp vinegar

Instructions:

1. Cook lentils and rice together in one pot.
2. Cook macaroni separately, then mix with the rice and lentils.
3. Sauté onions in olive oil until crispy and set aside.
4. In the same pan, cook garlic, cumin, and red pepper flakes, then add tomato sauce and vinegar. Simmer for 10 minutes.
5. Serve rice-lentil mix topped with sauce and crispy onions.

Spätzle (German Egg Noodles)

Ingredients:

- 2 cups flour
- ½ tsp salt
- ¼ tsp nutmeg (optional)
- 2 eggs
- ½ cup milk
- 1 tbsp butter

Instructions:

1. Mix flour, salt, and nutmeg in a bowl.
2. Add eggs and milk, stirring until a sticky dough forms.
3. Bring a pot of salted water to a boil.
4. Using a spätzle maker or colander, push dough through into boiling water.
5. Cook until noodles float, then drain and toss with butter.

Venezuelan Tallarines with Meat Sauce

Ingredients:

- 8 oz spaghetti or fettuccine
- 1 tbsp olive oil
- ½ lb ground beef
- 1 small onion, chopped
- 2 garlic cloves, minced
- 1 can (14 oz) crushed tomatoes
- 1 tsp cumin
- ½ tsp oregano
- Salt and pepper to taste
- ¼ cup grated Parmesan

Instructions:

1. Cook pasta and set aside.
2. Heat oil in a pan, then brown the beef.
3. Add onions and garlic, cook until soft.
4. Stir in tomatoes, cumin, oregano, salt, and pepper. Simmer for 15 minutes.
5. Serve over pasta and top with Parmesan.

Peruvian Tallarines Verdes (Green Spaghetti)

Ingredients:

- 8 oz spaghetti
- 2 cups fresh spinach
- 1 cup fresh basil
- ½ cup evaporated milk
- ¼ cup Parmesan cheese
- 2 tbsp olive oil
- 1 garlic clove
- ½ tsp red pepper flakes
- Salt and pepper to taste

Instructions:

1. Cook spaghetti and set aside.
2. Blend spinach, basil, evaporated milk, Parmesan, oil, garlic, and red pepper flakes until smooth.
3. Pour over hot pasta and toss to combine.

Tunisian Lablabi with Noodles

Ingredients:

- 1 tbsp olive oil
- 1 small onion, chopped
- 2 garlic cloves, minced
- 1 tsp harissa paste
- ½ tsp ground cumin
- ½ tsp paprika
- 1 can (14 oz) chickpeas, drained
- 3 cups vegetable broth
- 4 oz broken spaghetti or short pasta
- 1 tbsp lemon juice
- 1 poached egg (per serving, optional)

Instructions:

1. Heat oil and sauté onions and garlic.
2. Stir in harissa, cumin, and paprika.
3. Add chickpeas and broth, simmer for 15 minutes.
4. Add pasta and cook until tender.
5. Serve with lemon juice and a poached egg on top.